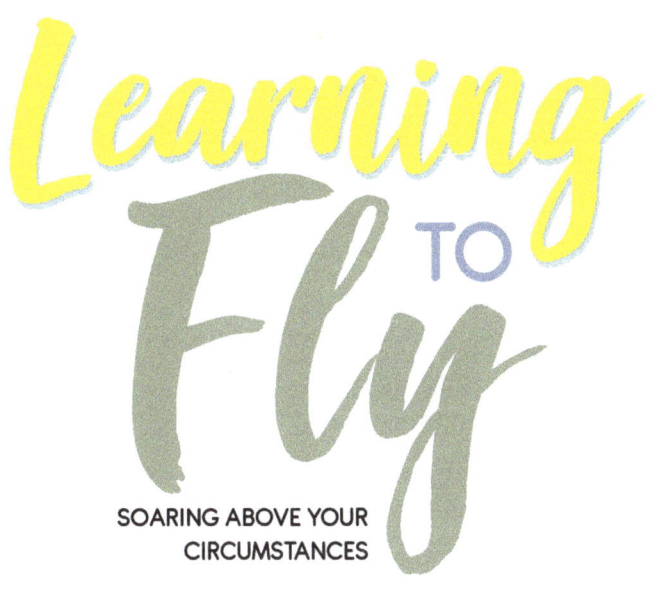

Learning to Fly

SOARING ABOVE YOUR CIRCUMSTANCES

PAMELA GOSS

LEARNING TO FLY
Copyright © 2025 by Pamela Goss

All rights reserved. Neither this publication nor any part of this publication may be reproduced or transmitted in any form or by any means, electronic or mechanical, including photocopying, recording or any information storage and retrieval system, without permission in writing from the author.

Scripture quotations marked (TPT) are from The Passion Translation®. Copyright © 2017, 2018, 2020 by Passion & Fire Ministries, Inc. Used by permission. All rights reserved. ThePassionTranslation.com. Scripture quotations marked (NIV) are taken from the Holy Bible, New International Version®, NIV®. Copyright © 1973, 1978, 1984, 2011 by Biblica, Inc.™ Used by permission of Zondervan. All rights reserved worldwide. www.zondervan.com The "NIV" and "New International Version" are trademarks registered in the United States Patent and Trademark Office by Biblica, Inc.™ Scripture quotations marked (TLB) are taken from The Living Bible, copyright © 1971 by Tyndale House Foundation. Used by permission of Tyndale House Publishers, Carol Stream, Illinois 60188. All rights reserved. Scripture quotations marked (NLT) are taken from the Holy Bible, New Living Translation, copyright ©1996, 2004, 2015 by Tyndale House Foundation. Used by permission of Tyndale House Publishers, Carol Stream, Illinois 60188. All rights reserved.

ISBN: 978-1-4866-2585-7
eBook ISBN: 978-1-4866-2586-4

Word Alive Press
119 De Baets Street Winnipeg, MB R2J 3R9
www.wordalivepress.ca

Cataloguing in Publication information can be obtained from Library and Archives Canada.

TO MY
chosen daughter
Emma,
MY GIRL, WHO I
love
TO THE
moon AND *back*.

I am so glad you came!

But those who trust in the Lord will find new strength. They will soar high on wings like eagles. They will run and not grow weary. They will walk and not faint. (Isaiah 40:31, NLT)

INTRODUCTION

AT TIMES DURING life's journey, we may walk through the valley of the shadow of death, but we do not walk through it alone. God is with us every step of the way, guiding and comforting us so we aren't overwhelmed by grief or consumed by fear. Friends and family come alongside as well, to sustain us until we pass through the darkness and come into the light again.

Oh but how we change! These trials occur not by fluke, for they are sent by God for our benefit, perfectly designed by his loving hand to take us higher. As we trust him, he fills us with his peace so we can soar above our circumstances. He is the wind beneath our wings.

> …he who began a good work in you will carry it on to completion until the day of Christ Jesus. (Philippians 1:6, NIV)

God loves us unfailingly and we can trust him with our lives as he does this good work, glorious, beneficial, excellent, and profitable.

In the summer of 2020, while the world was fighting COVID-19, I suddenly found myself in unbearable pain. I thought I was having a heart attack, so my husband John rushed me to the emergency room.

After getting an electrocardiogram, the doctor told me that he could see nothing wrong and I should go home.

Although I suffer from chronic pain due to post-polio syndrome, I knew this pain was very different.

Hours later, still in excruciating pain, we returned to the hospital. Still not knowing what was causing the pain, the doctor admitted me. It wasn't until I had a room that I received some strong pain medication and I was able to get some rest.

My admission marked the beginning of thirteen days of COVID isolation. I could have absolutely no visitors.

Thankfully, I didn't have COVID.

This also marked the beginning of numerous tests during my stay. Over the next several weeks, the doctors attempted to discover the source of my pain.

At first the doctors seemed certain that I had pancreatitis, which can be caused by alcohol abuse. However, I assured the doctor that I rarely drank any alcohol. Smiling, I told my nurse the same thing, knowing that the doctor didn't believe me.

A few days later, however, the doctor concluded that it wasn't pancreatitis after all.

In this book, I share my experiences based on the journal I kept at the time.

I love you.

JULY 21: Today I am praying using an excerpt from my previous book, *Songs in the Night*:

> Lord, you know what's on my heart. As I face this newest trial, it feels overwhelming and heart-breaking, but I know you are with me. I bring it to the foot of the cross and lay it down at your feet and trust you to work it all out for good.

JULY 22: Sometimes in life we face trial after trial. Yesterday, I had a lung biopsy after spending a week in the hospital suffering severe pain. Then my lung collapsed and I had to have a chest tube inserted while awake.

But then, God. In this storm, there he was, supporting me and helping me to be calm. Even the doctor and nurses commented on how calm I was. As the storm grew all around me, God said, "Take courage. It is I."

JULY 23: That evening, the doctor came to my bedside and told me I had either stage three or stage four lung cancer. Well, what do you do and say when someone tells you, "It's cancer"? The big C. For this, I have Jesus! Complete peace filled me and I knew that I wasn't alone.

Will it be stage three or stage four? One may be curable, the other not. The way ahead is unknown and dark.

Take my hand, Lord, and with your help I can handle whatever comes. With joy? Yes, even joy.

JULY 24: What a day! I've had my third biopsy. My lung half-collapsed again and now I will face more scans. You might say, "Let's not repeat that day."

But there was also joy today, from family, friends, and even strangers!

LEARNING TO FLY

I value you.

I received a beautiful bouquet from my son and family, as well as cards to let me know people care. A dear friend gave me a soothing lavender oil and many people called me on the phone, which was a wonderful surprise.

A nurse, at the end of her shift, took me to the hospital's rooftop garden. This was very special, as patients weren't supposed to leave their rooms because of COVID.

Then a sweet senior man who had been my roommate spoke some lovely words to me as he left for home.

And of course I received so many wonderful messages via social media.

Yes, I think I'll keep this day in my heart as one of the best during my hospital stay.

Waking up one morning, I was upset to discover that I had shingles, in addition to my daily dose of nausea. This was one other way in which my body was handling all the stress and medications.

JULY 25: Something I've been doing every day is reciting Psalm 23. I love how it presents a picture of Jesus as our good shepherd. He lovingly and tenderly cares for us each day and leads us to good places, providing for our needs along the way.

He knows his sheep intimately. This word, "know," comes from the Greek *ginosko*, which means recognizing and perceiving. It carries the idea of heart knowledge.

I love that Jesus really knows my heart and it is safe with him. He loves me unfailingly. When hard times come, when I walk through the valley of death, he takes my hand and goes with me. He binds up our wounds, healing and strengthening us, helping us to persevere, come what may.

One thing that made this time more difficult was not being able to have any visitors, including my husband.

One night I heard a man crying out for someone to read the Bible to him. He was in the long-term senior care room next to mine. How I would have loved to read scripture passages to him! Although COVID prevented me from doing so, some of the nurses did read to him when they had time.

JULY 26: I'm waiting this morning to see if I can be discharged from the hospital and go home. I have a very big battle to fight, but I also have an all-powerful God who will fight alongside me and I can trust his plan for my life.

I had thought that if I ever got a cancer diagnosis, I would be overcome with grief, but it's not so. God has filled me with his grace to handle it. I am able to calmly ask questions. I have grace, right when I need it. Oh, how my Saviour loves me so!

I will heal you.

> But the Lord will be the Savior of all who love
> him. Even in their time of trouble, God will live
> in them as strength. (Psalm 37:39, TPT)

JULY 27: I have been discharged! What a great way to celebrate my birthday. To mark the occasion, we went out for ice cream. I was so happy to be reunited with my husband and our sweet dog, Lucy!

Afterward, armed with three different morphine medications, we headed back to our island cottage on beautiful Lake Couchiching.

JULY 28: This morning, I was up with the dawn since the pain wouldn't let me sleep. What a glorious time of day! I watched as the sun came up and sparkled on the water. I noticed a solitary fisherman out enjoying the quiet morning.

While reading God's word, I thought about my time in the hospital and how I had taken my previous book, *Songs in the Night*, with me. One of the reasons I wrote that book was to comfort people in hospital—those who were in deep distress.

The prayers in that book did help me through my stay and sustained and comforted me. So in trying to help others, I too was helped. This is so often the case.

A dear friend who volunteers in many ways speaks of the joy she gets in reaching out to others. Her face lights up as she shares her experiences. I think she is the one who is most greatly blessed as she gives in every way she can, pouring out the love of Christ from the love he gives her.

JULY 29: Lord, I need your sustaining power today. Constant pain can lead to despair as I cry to you for release. I know you are here upholding me and carrying me. I will keep focused on you and your love for me. You are changing me through this pain, taking me to a deeper intimacy with you. My inner self is being renewed day by day. Renew a steadfast spirit within me and I will rest on your very great and precious promises. You give me abundant life even in my weakened state. I trust your deliverance for you make me strong.

> You are my hiding place; you will protect me from trouble and surround me with songs of deliverance. (Psalm 32:7, NIV)

My daughter Marcia, who lives in Calgary, decided that she needed to come help me when I came home from the hospital, but this was risky due to COVID. She came anyway, with her two boys, and then isolated to make sure they were healthy.

I will turn your fear to trust.

I will intercede for you with the Father.

I was so thankful, because I was in rough shape. Taking strong pain medications had led me to vomit constantly. I felt very weak, but having family nearby was such a blessing. I got to spend lots of time with my grandsons, talking and reading and just loving them. They told me they were praying for me to be well again. My heart was so full.

JULY 30: This dark path I'm on right now has some wonderful bursts of light, like a recent call from our niece Tammy, offering love and support. Then there was the time when our friend Angie came to our door with delicious food, or when Hilary called each day to lighten the load. Another day, I received a beautiful bouquet of flowers. And of course my husband supported me through everything.

All these acts of love push away the darkness and light up my world. So no matter what's happening, I feel strengthened to fight and gain victory over this cancer. These cheerleaders are gifts straight from the heart of Jesus.

Marcia took me to Sunnybrook Hospital one day for a PET scan. That's about a two-hour drive. While in Toronto, she visited with her brother Ben and his family while I had my appointment. To keep me protected, my family constantly checked themselves for signs of COVID, which was rampant at the time. The end result is that I enjoyed having a day out with Marcia and two of my grandchildren.

JULY 31: Someone once said, "Sometimes we need someone to simply be there—not to fix anything or to do anything in particular, but just to let us feel that we are cared for and supported."

Even during COVID, people showed me the truth of this by saying, "I'm praying for you." That meant everything to me. I felt loved and cared for by them, as if they were right there next to me in person.

When you're really ill, it's hard to pray very much. I had peace knowing that others were taking my needs to Jesus.

AUGUST 1: What a beautiful sunset tonight! And tomorrow, I know the sun will rise and set again. How faithful God is to always keep his creation orbiting as it should. We don't have to hope and pray for that; God keeps the universe in order.

My heavenly Father never leaves me to handle things alone. He is right here, leading and guiding, comforting and sustaining, supplying my needs at just the perfect time.

There are so many unknowns in my life right now, but I know that God, with his hand in mine, will help me go forward with confidence.

LEARNING TO FLY

I will uphold you.

AUGUST 2: What do we do when we find ourselves in a desperate situation? One thing is for sure: we need God's help.

The Israelites found themselves in a hopeless situation while wandering the desert. They had no more water for themselves or their animals. What was the answer? God told them to fill the valley with ditches that he would then fill with water.

As we wait for God's answer, we need to fill our minds with his word, because Satan will come along and whisper negative, untrue things in our ears. Make sure there's no sin to hinder your prayers. To keep your spirits up, sing praises and listen to praise music. Pray Psalm 29, for it speaks of how majestic and powerful God is. Then wait for the victory with joy in your heart.

AUGUST 3: It has been said, "Time is like a river. You cannot touch the same water twice because the flow that has passed will never pass again." So enjoy every moment of your life.

LEARNING TO FLY

I will take hold of your hand.

I will help you.

AUGUST 6: My PET scan showed cancer in the lymph nodes under my arms, which is where I feel a lot of my pain. I will be having a lung biopsy in Toronto with Dr. Saffiedine, a specialist who will investigate the lump that has been found in my right lung.

AUGUST 7: Even though I'm just starting this cancer journey, I know that I don't walk my path alone. Jesus walks with me, and sometimes he even carries me. We live in a fallen world and must face trials—but as the trials increase, so does his grace.

We are told not to worry, and even to rejoice, because God will use our hard times to bring about the good. The coming journey will change me, and as I trust him with my life others may just decide to walk with Jesus, too.

In the night, when the pain doesn't let me rest, God's presence feels very real. He is alive and so full of love and care for me. He doesn't leave me to suffer alone. We have a God who sees, hears, and acts on our behalf, because he *lives*.

AUGUST 8: As Moses and the Israelites were being pursued by Pharaoh and his army, they found themselves trapped against the shores of the Red Sea with nowhere to turn except to God. God parted the sea, providing dry ground for the Israelites to escape and pass over to the other side.

Wow! That is God, for he always goes the extra mile. I can imagine the Israelites' hearts beating wildly as they hurried across to safety.

As the last foot touched the opposite shore, God let the water come crashing down, destroying Pharaoh and the more than six hundred chariots and their riders. In fact, many bones and chariot parts have been discovered at the bottom of the Red Sea.

That is the God I serve. He is so merciful and compassionate to our cries for help. But we do suffer, and I believe that God uses this suffering to mature us. At the right time, he will deliver us for his glory.

God could take all the pain away, but I know there is a bigger picture I cannot see. He is fulfilling his purpose and I trust him with my life.

> We've passed through fire and flood, yet in the end you always bring us out better than we were before, saturated with your goodness. (Psalm 66:12, TPT)

LEARNING TO FLY

I will strengthen you.

AUGUST 10: Today I was hospitalized in order to have a chest tube removed from my right lung. Praise God! Around this same time, I received an encouraging message from a friend in Africa. Another friend had filled her in about my situation and she wanted me to know that she was praying. How awesome is that?

I have been amazed at the support that has flowed in from my friends in the Lord. They are so willing to lift me up in prayer. My natural family has rallied around me, too, helping in so many ways. Especially touching is my sweet grandson Joey, eight years of age, who told me that he is praying for me to be better. All this outpouring of love makes such a difference!

AUGUST 12: One of my favourite authors is Barbara Johnson, who suffered much in this life. Her husband was in a near-fatal accident, suffering debilitating injuries. Two of her sons died, one in Vietnam and another to a drunk driver. A common theme of her books is that pain is inevitable but misery is optional.[1]

I have sat in quite a few waiting rooms lately and come to appreciate the people who make the time go faster by striking up a conversation. I also appreciate those special

---

[1] Barbara Johnson, *Stick a Geranium in Your Hat and Be Happy* (Dallas, TX: Word Publishing, 1990).

nurses and doctors who joke with their patients. It really takes the sting out of one's circumstances.

Barbara taught me to always look for the humour in a situation. We can be God's voice to those who are hurting, encouraging and brightening up their day. A little humour never hurts.

> ...I have hope: because of the Lord's great love we are not consumed, for his compassions never fail. They are new every morning; great is your faithfulness. (Lamentations 3:21–23, NIV)

AUGUST 13: God's love is unfailing. These days are hard, but I always place myself in his hands of love. This is the God who sent his only son, Jesus, to come and show us how much he loves us. This is the Saviour who willingly paid the cost of my sin and yours and so longs for us to become part of his family. He is the way, the truth, and the life! He is love! I can trust in a God like that! He is my healer.

I will shelter you.

AUGUST 14: I recently had a lymph node biopsy. So many people are praying for me, which gives me such courage and strength to face another painful test.

When I got to my appointment, the nurse informed me that they wouldn't perform a biopsy if the indications didn't point to cancer. This made me very anxious.

When the doctor started, he and the nurse had lots of lymph nodes to choose from. At the end of the procedure, the doctor told me to get myself to a lung specialist. I felt assured, since at least I already had one in Dr. N. Saffiedine at Michael Garron Hospital in Toronto.

I find so much comfort in the Psalms. I have been claiming this promise: *"Sustain me, my God, according to your promise, and I will live; do not let my hopes be dashed. Uphold me, and I will be delivered..."* (Psalm 119:116, NIV)

AUGUST 15: Someone who had terminal cancer once said, "Don't be sad for me. We all come to this world to be tourists, to enjoy life and go sightseeing. I just happen to be leaving earlier than others."

AUGUST 16: My one-year-old grandson Leo shouts "Come, come" when he wants someone. This reminds me of how our Lord says, "Come and fellowship with me."

As I pour out my heart to God, I find the strength to go on. I am assured of his love and feel his peace even while facing this cancer. Each day seems to bring new challenges, but I know that I don't walk this journey alone.

Lately I faced rejection from someone close to me. I felt abandoned just when I needed support. But people will let you down sometimes, and that's why we must keep our eyes on Jesus and rest on his promises. I will forgive, because God has forgiven me of so much. He will never turn away but lovingly keep me in his care. How wonderful is that?

AUGUST 20: In every situation, God is with me. His name is Immanuel, which means "God with you." This is true even amidst my cancer trial. Jesus is providing all I need to get through and be victorious. Thankfulness fills my heart as I look to him for support and to gain wisdom to make the right choices for my treatment. My life is in his hands. That's a very secure place to be.

AUGUST 23: To avoid falling into despair and discouragement, I have been trying to keep my mind focused on Jesus. I look for the blessings he sends each day.

I will rescue you.

I will lift you up.

For example, I think of my husband of forty-five years as of today, who has supported me through my sickness. I think of the looks of love I get from my daughter. I think of the warm hugs from my grandchildren. I think of my tomato plant, full of tomatoes even though it's been sadly neglected. I think of the beauty of an orchid. I think of the joy of being outside again after almost two weeks in the hospital. I think of a friend who calls every day. I think of my beautiful daughter-in-law, who cooks delicious food to tempt me to eat.

Each day, there is so much beauty to discover, when I open my eyes to see. I choose to be full of gratitude for the blessings upon blessings in my life.

AUGUST 27: On this rainy day, I spent the morning at the cancer clinic. The doctor tells me that I'll need to go to Toronto for a lung scope. This should finally confirm whether I have lung cancer.

As I sit in the waiting room, I watch people come and go. It breaks my heart to see all their pain and suffering. So I pray for each one. Good health is such a gift to treasure. I truly believe that my life is in God's hands, whatever the test reveals.

I will sustain you.

AUGUST 31: Everyone's prayers mean so much to me. I am truly lifted up each day and know that God is helping me. In 2 Corinthians 1, the apostle Paul writes about comfort. The Greek word for comfort, *paraklesis*, paints a picture of someone coming alongside another to encourage them in the midst of a severe trial. This is what people have done for me.

> I waited patiently for the Lord; he turned to me and heard my cry. He lifted me out of the slimy pit, out of the mud and mire; he set my feet on a rock and gave me a firm place to stand. (Psalm 40:1–2, NIV)

Truly, God has answered these prayers. At times of the day, I feel no nausea or great pain. I thank God for everyone, as well as his gracious gift of mercy.

SEPTEMBER 1: In my weakness, the Lord has become my strength. As I read in Psalm 18:2,

> You're as real to me as bedrock beneath my feet, like a castle on a cliff, my forever firm fortress, my mountain of hiding, my pathway of escape, my tower of rescue where none can reach me. My secret strength and

> shield around me, you are salvation's ray of
> brightness shining on the hillside, always the
> champion of my cause. (Psalm 18:2–3, TPT)

SEPTEMBER 22: When I was going through my biopsies, as the doctors looked for evidence of cancer, I learned how hard it is to wait for results. This fall is such an uncertain time for me.

God has a unique path for each of us and he promises to light our way. He says, "Trust me." In this trial, I am growing deeper in my faith and becoming more encased in Jesus's unfailing love for me.

> Your gracious Spirit is all I need, so lead me
> on good paths that are pleasing to you, my
> one and only God! (Psalm 143:10, TPT)

SEPTEMBER 23: As King Hezekiah was dying, he cried out to God and God healed him using a poultice of figs. To an Israelite, figs represent peace and divine favour. I love that God gave him extra assurance.

Our God is *"rich in compassion and mercy"* (Ephesians 2:4, TPT). He answers prayer and exhorts us to *"pray continually"* (1 Thessalonians 5:17, TPT). God will always answer according to his will. We can have peace in knowing that the answer is always for our best.

I am your Saviour.

Your arm is endued with power; your hand is strong, your right hand exalted. (Psalm 89:13, NIV)

SEPTEMBER 24: I used to live my live in the *if-only*. If only I had someone to love me. If only I was married. If only I had children.

I know you're chuckling at that one.

Though these wonderful happenings have enriched my life, I have learned that I need to enjoy each day as it comes. True joy comes from God, who fills me with his unfailing love and deep contentment. He will satisfy the deep longings of my heart.

Even with all the sickness I've felt this summer, Jesus has filled me with his loving presence so I have a deep feeling that everything will be worked out for my own good.

Charles Spurgeon has said, "Fiery trials make golden Christians."[2]

SEPTEMBER 25: Today, I am off to Toronto for the lung scope. God has me in his hands, I know.

---

[2] Charles H. Spurgeon, "Firey trials make golden Christians," Quotefancy.com. Date of access: July 19, 2024 (https://quotefancy.com/quote/786518/Charles-H-Spurgeon-Fiery-trials-make-golden-Christians).

LEARNING TO FLY

I am your peace.

> You have seen me tossing and turning through the night. You have collected all my tears and preserved them in your bottle! You have recorded every one in your book. (Psalm 56:8, TLB)

SEPTEMBER 26: These past weeks have been a period of suffering, with many painful biopsies and uncertainties. But it has also been a time of inner growth, with God showering me with his love. He has been doing a necessary work on me, stretching me to the limit. His word says that he is making us into a masterpiece, one day at a time.

I have also been shown so much love by family and friends who have taken the time to care and be supportive. It's a summer I will never forget. We don't need to be afraid to suffer, for in our suffering we grow strong and courageous and see that God is for us!

SEPTEMBER 27: Does God promise us a rose garden filled with nothing but sunny days? No. In fact, God says that in this life we will have trouble. But Jesus also promises that he will never leave us; he will give us strength to handle whatever comes. We just need to put our trust in him and not waste our time worrying and fussing.

God has promised to light our paths and provide wisdom to make the right decisions. We will have the strength of his inexhaustible right hand and the hope that he will come through for us at the right time and in his perfect plan.

Most wonderful of all is the promise that Jesus will bring good out of our circumstances. This is why God tells us to rejoice, because he's got our backs. We will have victory, for Jesus has overcome the world!

SEPTEMBER 28: My heart was saddened this morning, to hear of a husband and father who died from COVID. The man's wife is suffering, too, with the virus. Life can be overwhelming and sorrow all-encompassing. How fearful this couple's kids must be that they might lose their mom as well!

Jacob had lost all hope and was grief-stricken to think his favourite son had died. But on learning that Joseph was alive and governing all of Egypt, Jacob revived. The word revive refers to nourishing, restoring, recovering, repairing, and making something whole and alive again. We too can find life very hard and lose our will to live, but God can revive us.

I am always at work in your life.

> Revive me with your tender love and spare
> my life by your kindness, and I will continue
> to obey you. (Psalm 119:88, TPT)

These hopeful words from the Psalms are wonderful. They bring us back to life. We can pray them time after time. God will give us a fresh anointing of faith so we can both make it through and be made *"mature and complete, not lacking anything"* (James 1:4, NIV).

I am reminded of Shadrach, Meshach, and Abednego when they came out of the fiery furnace:

> ...the fire had not harmed their bodies, nor
> was a hair of their heads singed; their robes
> were not scorched, and there was no smell
> of fire on them. (Daniel 3:2, NIV)

> In all of my affliction I find great comfort in
> your promises, for they have kept me alive!
> (Psalm 119:50, TPT)

SEPTEMBER 29: It was John Newton who once wrote, "Remember the growth of a believer is not like a mushroom, but like an oak, which increases slowly indeed, but surely. Many suns, showers, and frosts pass upon it before it comes to perfection; and in winter, when it seems dead, it is gathering strength at the root. Be humble, watchful, and diligent in the means, and endeavour to look through all, and fix your eye upon Jesus, and all shall be well."[3]

SEPTEMBER 30: We can be certain that whatever God sends into our lives has first passed through his filter. Nothing comes into the life of a Christian that God doesn't know about. Believing that, we can relax and know that he will be with us during the trials ahead.

Someone once said: "A meaningful life is not being rich, being popular, being highly educated or being perfect. It is about being real, being humble, being able to share ourselves and touch the lives of others. It is only then that we could have a full, happy and contented life."

OCTOBER 1: Just because we belong to God doesn't mean we will have a trouble-free life. In fact, we may have even more trouble, because we suffer as believers in Christ. We are told to count it all joy and not be surprised by the trials, for they come to us all.

---

[3] John Newton, "Letters of John Newton," *Thirdmill.org.* March 18, 1767 (https://thirdmill.org/magazine/article.asp/link/joh_newton%5Ejoh_newton.letters001.html/at/Letters%20of%20John%20Newton).

I am faithful.

But we do not bear them alone, for God is with us every step of our journey and he gives us promises to cling to.

> And the God of all grace, who called you to his eternal glory in Christ, after you have suffered a little while, will himself restore you and make you strong, firm and steadfast. (1 Peter 5:10, NIV)

I know of a woman named Karen, a single mom of three, who has been diagnosed with esophageal cancer. She had to have her esophagus removed. Afterward, the elders of her church had a special time of prayer and anointed her for healing. She believes in the power of prayer and many others have prayed as well, which means so much to her.

It has been a long, hard journey. She is well today but still can only eat small bites at a time.

"Do I wish I had never had cancer?" she said to me. "No. For in this journey, I have grown so much more intimate with my Saviour."

In the midst of our sufferings, we have hope!

> Love divine has seen and counted
> Every tear it caused to fall,

And the storm which love appointed,
Was its choicest gift of all.[4]

DECEMBER 18: Today, the specialist will call to confirm whether or not I have lung cancer. My good friends Beth and Catherine invited me over for lunch.

"We will celebrate with you if it's good news and cry with you if it's not," they said.

When the specialist called that morning, I could tell it was good news. He sounded very happy.

"There is no cancer in the lymph nodes," he reported. "In fact, it looks very healthy. But there is a small lump in the right lung that we will check in six months."

And if the test was still negative in six months, the next checkup would happen in a year. Relief flooded through my soul as I thanked him. I also thanked Jesus!

What a wonderful day I had with my friends! We had a delicious lunch followed by an afternoon of music, for they are both gifted musicians. I will always treasure this day.

---
[4] "Christ My Song," Jane Laurie Borthwick, 1550.

I am truth.

JANUARY 20: My morning started with a call from a friend. I shared with her the doctor's good news and that I felt God had healed me. This friend, though, had needed to go through many cancer treatments, even though she is cancer-free today.

It's so hard to understand why God heals some people right away and not others. Some are healed after getting to heaven. But he has a different path for each of us to follow and he always has our best interests at heart.

JANUARY 21: Today I talked with my friend Paula. I hadn't talked to her since before I was sick, probably the previous spring. She told me that she had heard I was sick but hadn't known with what. She had decided to pray for a miracle, for me to be completely healed. We just rejoiced together since God had answered by stepping in and completely healing me of cancer!

This is what it means to be in the family of God. There is so much love and care for each other. We gladly take each other's needs to Jesus and share in all the joys and sorrows of our lives. It sure makes our lives more fulfilling and worthwhile!

CONCLUSION

THE FOLLOWING YEAR in May, my sister-in-law had a tumour removed from her brain, and sadly she died shortly afterward. I also have known many others in my life who went through chemotherapy and radiation.

Cancer is so insidious and makes us focus on what really matters in life. So what does matter? It's not all our possessions; it's our faith, friends, and family.

For many years, I prayed for new windows for our cottage, since the wood was rotting and the glass was hard to see through. When we finally got those new windows, we could clearly see out of the glass again.

In other words, we could see what is most important.

God taught me many things through my illness, but most of all I learned to cherish my Saviour and those special people in my life.

Whatever we go through, God will bring good out of it. We can trust his plan for our lives. But for some, healing will only come when they pass into glory. I believe that when we get to heaven and see how wonderful it is, we will never look back.

> So here's what I learned through it all: leave all your cares and anxieties at the feet of the Lord, and measureless grace will strengthen you. (Psalm 55:22, TPT)

We can be at peace because we know that Jesus will never fail us. God is for us. He is on our side. We can trust in his great love for us to work everything together for our good. Joy comes when we discover that Christ is right there in the midst of our trials. He says,

> So do not fear, for I am with you; do not be dismayed, for I am your God. I will strengthen you and help you; I will uphold you with my righteous right hand. (Isaiah 41:10, NIV)

Someone once wrote, "When God pushes you to the edge, trust him fully, because only two things can happen: either he will catch you when you fall or he will teach you how to fly."

HOPE IS THE THING WITH FEATHERS

Hope is the thing with feathers
That perches in the soul,
And sings the tune without the words,
And never stops at all,

And sweetest in the gale is heard;
And sore must be the storm
That could abash the little bird
That kept so many warm.

I've heard it in the chillest land,
And on the strangest sea;
Yet, never, in extremity,
It asked a crumb of me.[5]

—Emily Dickinson

---

[5] Emily Dickinson, "Hope is the thing with feathers," *Poets.org*. Date of access: April 10, 2024 (https://poets.org/poem/hope-thing-feathers-254).

SONGS IN THE NIGHT
978-1-4866-1841-5

Your life can change in the blink of any eye. Unexpectedly, something happens that turns your world upside-down. You're blindsided and overwhelmed. It seems like you have a mountain to climb every day.

This book of prayers will help you through such a time, offering hope and encouragement. God is waiting to hear from you, to come alongside and give you strength. He cares about you and loves you deeply. Even in your darkest circumstances, there can be hope and even joy!

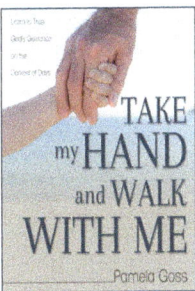

TAKE MY HAND AND WALK WITH ME
978-1-4866-1876-7

Sometimes along our journeys, we face a rough and rocky path. We cannot see clearly ahead and it's hard to keep persevering.

This is the time to take hold of God's right hand. He will travel with us, strengthening and guiding us, to a whole new destination—a place of abundance.

Come and discover the ways in which God will bless you when you take his hand in yours.

www.ingramcontent.com/pod-product-compliance
Lightning Source LLC
Chambersburg PA
CBHW041929090426
42743CB00021B/3479